Chip Davis'
DAY PARTS For

solo piano

CONTENTS

ISBN 0-7935-4690-7

Published by
DOTS AND LINES, INK

9130 MORMON BRIDGE ROAD OMAHA, NEBRASKA 68152 402.457.4341

EXCLUSIVELY DISTRIBUTED BY

HAL•LEONARD® CORPORATION

7777 W. BLUEMOUND RD. P.O. BOX 13819 MILWAUKEE, WI 53213

SUNDAY MORNING COFFEE

By CHIP DAVIS

Gently rhythmic

With pedal

SILVER SCREEN ROMANCE

By MICHAEL HOPPÉ

COFFEE WITH CARLA

By JOHN ARCHER

16

MAINE COURSE

By JACKSON BERKEY

20

22

(keep pedal)

(keep pedal)

mp *mf*

senza Ped. *(repeat fingering)*
slowly add pedal-------

------------------- to full Ped. *(keep pedal)*

(keep pedal)

Ped. *Ped.*

SHAMELESS CHEF

By CHIP DAVIS

molto rall.

12

PARTY AT DOMENICO'S
SONATA IN D MAJOR
Domenico Scarlatti (1685 - 1757)

Edited and Annotated by
JACKSON BERKEY

SPIDER MONKEY

By JEFF JENKINS

SCOTTY'S BARBEQUE

By MIKE POST

With a steady beat

8vb -

loco

8vb - - - - - - - - - - - - - -

loco

Repeat ad lib. and Fade

SHINING BY THE RIVER

By RICHARD BURMER

Unhurried and lyrical

With pedal

Repeat and Fade

ON THE EDGE OF FOREVER

By JOHN ARCHER
and RON SATTERFIELD

Play 3 times, ad lib.

CHILDREN'S WALTZ THEME

By MICHAEL HOPPÉ

Simply (♩ = 96)

Use pedal sparingly

Play 3 times and Fade

KANBAI

By CHIP DAVIS

D.C. al Coda
(with repeat)

CODA